The Management Map...

Companion Workbook

Deborah Avrin, MS, SPHR

ManageSmart Publishing

This publication contains the opinions and ideas of the author. The author and publisher specifically disclaim all responsibility for any liability, loss, or risk, personal or otherwise, that is incurred as a consequence, directly or indirectly, of the uses and applications of this book. Any and all implied or expressed warranties of fitness are hereby disclaimed.

Published by ManageSmart Publishing
Plano, Texas
972-881-5282

Printed in the United States of America

ISBN: 978-0-9820901-1-4

Cover design: MC2 Graphics

To Erica Avrin, a champion of *The Management Map*

and my special daughter.

Contents

Acknowledgments   vii

Introduction   ix

Chapter One: Visualizing Your Management Map   1-2

1. Create Your Management Vision   3-4
2. Three C's of Management   5-6
3. Become a Role Model   7
4. Avoid New Manager Traps   8
5. Assess Your Style   9
6. Assess Managerial Competencies   10
7. Build Managerial Competencies   11

Chapter Two: Navigating Company Expectations   13-14

1. Create Your Management Travel Guidebook   15
2. Use Your Management Travel Guidebook   16-17
3. The Expectations Meeting   18-19
4. Workplace Attire   20

Chapter Three: Getting to Know Your Traveling Companions   21-22

1. Get to Know Your Team Members   23-24
2. Create a Team Snapshot   25

Chapter Four: No Manager Is an Island   27-28

1. Collaboration Activity Part A   29
2. Collaboration Activity Part B   30
3. Understand Your Customers   31-32
4. Develop Customer Empathy   33
5. Establish Vendor Expectations   34
6. Analyze the Competition   35

Chapter Five: Setting Your Course and Speed   37-38

1. Goals of the Organization   39
2. Goal Setting for Your Department   40
3. Involve Your Team in Goal Setting   41-42
4. Establish Expectations for Your Team   43-44

Chapter Six: Opening Communication Channels   45-46

1. Establish Meeting Agendas   47
2. Examine Meeting Roles   48-49
3. Choose a Communication Channel   50

Chapter Seven: Guiding the Journey   51-52

1. Rate Your Work Climate   53
2. Improve Your Work Climate   54
3. Examine Your Thoughts   55
4. Rate Your Coaching Skills   56
5. Practice Coaching I   57-59
6. Practice Coaching II   60-61

Chapter Eight: Getting There on Time   63-64

1. Complete a Time Log   65-67
2. Analyze Your Time Log   68-69
3. Project Planning   70-71

Chapter Nine: License to Manage   73-74

1. Review Federal Agency Websites   75
2. Respond to Employee Situations   76-77
3. Practice Employee Situations   78

Chapter Ten: Navigating Roadblocks, Detours, and Speed Bumps   79-80

1. Navigate a Roadblock   81-82
2. Analyze an Organizational Change   83-84
3. Analyze Conflict Situation   85

Final Activity: Action Plan   87

Additional Resources for Your Management Journey   89

Acknowledgments

A question and an experiment.... Could a human resources professional conduct a training class using *The Management Map: Navigation Tools for the New Manager*? A request for volunteers to participate in the experiment yielded three volunteers. Without their ideas and willingness to contribute, the birth of *The Management Map Companion Workbook* would not have been possible. I gratefully acknowledge their contributions. Here are their stories:

The first to raise their hands were Judy Martin Human Resource Manager and Michael Nelson, Facility Manager at IRIS USA, Inc. Mike said, "We need a workbook." "A workbook?" I said in surprise. "Can't people just write down the answers to the activity questions at the end of each chapter?" Judy and Mike both felt that people would want a structured workbook for recording their thoughts and answers. Mike explained, "I might loan the book to someone, but the workbook I'll keep for myself because it contains my personal reflections." When I asked the two other volunteers, they had the same reaction, so the *Companion Workbook* was born.

Judy conducted two sessions for her first and second shift supervisors, approximately six people in each class, held once a week for ten weeks. Several attendees did not speak English as their first language, so she completed many of the activities as group discussions. She related each activity to a situation that had recently occurred in the workplace to make the content relevant.

Second up was Jasmine Wilder, HR Manager at Goody Goody Liquor. Jasmine had three recently promoted managers and one new manager to the company who attended. She held the classes over six weeks; the first week spent on an introduction and chapter one and then two chapters a week thereafter. Some activities were assigned as pre or post work and some were done in class. Jasmine added her own creativity by asking for a copy of what the participants wrote from the first activity, "Create your management vision," to be mailed to them one year after the class. She created slides to guide the discussion.

Lastly, Barbara Adkins, Corporate Training Manager for Graphic Solutions Group, Inc., tested the book. Barbara had a unique situation in that out of a selected audience of four people, two worked out of town. She conducted the training via a webinar and also added PowerPoint slides to keep participants focused. She conducted the training over 12 one-hour sessions. A unique approach Barbara added was built-in coaching by participant's managers who also had a book and workbook they used to follow along with their progress.

I offer my sincere gratitude to Judy, Mike, Jasmine, and Barbara. As a result of their efforts *The Management Map Companion Workbook* is a much better learning tool.

A terrific team of professionals also contributed to the successful completion of this book: cover designer Alan McCuller, editor Martha McCuller, and coaching friend Fiona Hunter.

Introduction

Many people keep a travel journal when they go on a journey. The purpose of travel journals are to record experiences and preserve memories. Travelers realize their journey is about what they are seeing and hearing and also about what they are thinking and feeling. A natural follow-up to the book *The Management Map: Navigation Tools for the New Manager* is this *Companion Workbook*, which serves as your travel journal during your management journey.

After you read each chapter, turn to the matching section in *The Management Map Companion Workbook*. Each section begins with a summary of the chapter to provide you with a refresher of key concepts. The activities in the chapter and additional focus activities are listed for you to track your progress on activity outcomes. The workbook contains over 40 activities. You can complete all the activities or just pick and choose those most relevant for your position.

Allow about one to one and half hours to complete the activities for each chapter. Each session begins with the following questions:
- What did you like best about the chapter? What topic resonated with you?
- Which concepts in the chapter apply to your department or organization?
- Which quote did you like from the chapter?

Suggested uses for this book include:
- **Self study** — For those managers who prefer to learn on their own. You can reflect on the concepts alone or locate a coach or accountability partner to provide you with someone to discuss ideas and concepts.
- **Coaching** — *The Management Map* and the *Companion Workbook* are great tools for coaching managers one-on-one. Simply assign chapters and then conduct your coaching sessions around the concepts and how to apply them in their positions.
- **Self directed study groups** — A study group can act like a book club. Locate a small group of people who are in similar job positions and create a meeting schedule. Group members can take turns facilitating discussions during the sessions.
- **Facilitator-led workshops** — Facilitators can invite a number of participants and use the *Companion Workbook* in a workshop setting. You can customize the learning experience by adding your company's philosophy, policies, and procedures to the activities.

The act of writing things down helps reinforce concepts and adds them to your long term memory. Using *The Management Map Companion Workbook* will increase your retention of the knowledge and skills you are gaining.

Enjoy your management journey and your new travel journal.

ONE

VISUALIZING YOUR MANAGEMENT MAP...
How Will You Go?

Objectives:
- Create your management vision
- Identify your managerial competencies

The Management Map **Reference Pages:** 1-18

Chapter Summary:
The chapter begins with a story of John, who is retiring. A number of John's former team members and managers have wonderful things to say at his retirement party. The book poses the question to new managers, "If this were your retirement party, what would your former employees and managers comment about you? What comments would you like to hear?"

New managers are then asked to create their own management vision by answering several questions. Vision statements can be written or displayed on a vision board.

Managers need to transition away from their previous roles as individual contributors. There are a number of perspective shifts to make, and there are traps that new managers encounter. When making the transition, it is important to be true to oneself. Strengths may be examined from a managerial perspective by using a behavior assessment tool such as Inscape Publishing's DiSC® profile.

The chapter concludes with a description of typical managerial competencies and instructions on how to create a development plan to build these skills.

Your Initial Reflection:
What did you like best about the chapter? What topic resonated with you?

_____

_____

_____

Which concepts in the chapter apply to your department or organization?

_____

_____

_____

Which quote did you like from the chapter?

_____

_____

_____

Journey Progress — Check after you complete each activity:

❏ **Activity 1.1: Create Your Management Vision** — By answering reflection questions, you will be able to craft a vision of the type of manager you want to become.

❏ **Activity 1.2: The Three C's of Management** — Develop plans to build your confidence, competence and courage as a manager.

❏ **Activity 1.3: Become a Role Model** — Analyze the characteristics of other managers to determine the attributes you would like to emulate as a manager.

❏ **Activity 1.4: Avoid New Manager Traps** — Examine typical new manager traps and develop a plan to avoid them.

❏ **Activity 1.5: Assess Your Style** — Take a behavior style assessment such as DiSC to examine how to use your strengths as a manager.

❏ **Activity 1.6: Assess Managerial Competencies** — Review a list of managerial competencies and rate your proficiency.

❏ **Activity 1.7: Build Managerial Competencies** — Chose several managerial competencies and plan developmental activities.

Activity 1.1

Create Your Management Vision
The Management Map reference pages 3-6

It is your retirement party... your management journey is ending. What will people say about you?

_____

_____

_____

Activity Directions: Picture the manager you want to be while you answer the following questions. You will then be ready to write a managerial vision statement.

1. Why did you become a manager?

_____

_____

2. What strengths do you see in yourself? What have others said about your strengths?

_____

_____

3. What are several of your critical values? Examples: Integrity, teamwork, results, interaction, etc.

_____

_____

4. When your management career is ending, what will you regret not doing, seeing, or achieving?

_____

_____

Activity 1.1 Continued

Reflect on your answers to the questions on the previous page. Use the space below to create your managerial vision. Write the statements as if you are already making them happen in your life. Some experts recommend 50 words or less. Suggested opening can be "I am the type of manager who..."

_____

_____

_____

_____

_____

_____

_____

_____

_____

_____

_____

_____

_____

Share your vision with others and get feedback until you feel it is clear and a good reflection of what you want to be as a manager.

Rewrite it on a paper or card and put it where you can periodically reflect on your vision. When you are struggling with a decision or path you need to take in your management journey, review your vision statement.

We can all make a conscious choice to become a great manager!

Activity 1.2

The Three C's of Management
The Management Map reference pages 6-7

Activity Directions: Making the transition means developing the three C's of Management: Confidence, Competence, and Courage. Complete the following about the three C's:

Develop **Confidence** to perform your management role while being true to your vision.
1. Why is it important to be confident as a manager?

_____

_____

_____

2. How can you develop confidence as a manager?

_____

_____

_____

Develop **Competence** in using your skills and abilities to perform your role, while continuing to seek opportunities for continued improvement.
1. Why is it important to be competent as a manager?

_____

_____

_____

2. How can you develop competence as a manager?

_____

_____

_____

Activity 1.2 Continued

Develop **Courage** to make the right decisions and not just the popular or easy decisions.
1. Why is it important to have courage as a manager?

_____

_____

_____

2. How can you develop courage as a manager?

_____

_____

_____

Activity 1.3

Become a Role Model
The Management Map reference pages 9-10

Activity Directions: Managers are role models in the organization. We can learn how to be a better role model from reflecting on our past experiences. First reflect on the managers you've had in the past and what you can learn from them.

1. What does being a role model mean to you?

_____

_____

_____

2. Describe the best manager(s) you have ever had.

_____

_____

_____

3. What strengths would you like to emulate from this manager?

_____

_____

_____

4. Describe the worst manager(s) you have ever had.

_____

_____

_____

5. What negative characteristics would you like to avoid?

_____

_____

_____

Activity 1.4

Avoid New Manager Traps
The Management Map reference pages 7-9

Activity Directions: You have been given the responsibility and the power of authority based on your new managerial position. When managers are unsure of how to handle their new authority, they may fall into traps. Review the following typical new manager traps and the impact of each of the behaviors. Then, create an action plan on how to avoid one of the traps.

1. Check which traps you may likely fall into as a manager:

    ☐ **Carrot and Stick** — Managers who believe that to get team members to do something they must either offer an incentive (a carrot) or threaten (with a stick)
    What are the long-term consequences of this behavior?

    ☐ **Apologetic** — Instead of being comfortable with their authority, managers apologize when giving instructions or requests
    What are the long-term consequences of this behavior?

    ☐ **Buddy and Pal** — Managers who are promoted from within and now have to supervise the same people who used to be coworkers have difficulty adapting to their new role
    What are the long-term consequences of this behavior?

    ☐ **Do-It-Myself** — When managers prefer to do tasks themselves rather than delegate or coach others to take on tasks
    What are the long-term consequences of this behavior?

2. Pick one of the traps and list ideas and plans on how you will avoid it.

    _____

    _____

    _____

Activity 1.5

Assess Your Style
The Management Map reference pages 10-11

Activity Directions: Take a behavioral assessment such as Inscape Publishing's DiSC®. After you review your results, answer the following questions:

1. What are your style strengths related to being a manager?

_____

_____

_____

2. How does the feedback from your profile mesh with your managerial vision statement?

_____

_____

_____

3. What style characteristics might hinder your effectiveness as a manager?

_____

_____

_____

4. Pick three to six of your style strengths. How they can assist you to become a more effective manager?

Strength	How It Can Be Utilized

Activity 1.6

Assess Managerial Competencies
The Management Map **reference pages 11-13**

Activity Directions: There are many competencies that managers use every day. Some may be very natural for you, others may need more development. Assess your current skill level in the following managerial competencies; add competencies specific for your organization.

Competency	Proficient	Experienced	Intermediate	Beginner
1. Administrating policies and procedures				
2. Implementing the company vision, mission, and values				
3. Building relationships with your team members				
4. Collaborating with other line and staff positions				
5. Setting goals and expectations				
6. Coaching your team members				
7. Communicating and listening				
8. Managing your time, planning, and prioritizing				
9. Understanding employment law				
10. Solving problems				
11. Managing change				
12. Resolving conflict				
13.				

Activity 1.7

Build Managerial Competencies
The Management Map reference pages 13-14

Activity Directions: After understanding the competencies required for your position and assessing your current skill level, it is time to plan how you will further develop your competencies. An effective development plan will include activities you will complete for your development and a target date for completion.

Development Activity Ideas:
- Reading — books, articles
- Mentoring/coaching
- Training workshop
- e-learning
- Project
- Task force participation
- Internet research
- Best practice search

From the competency list you developed, list each competency, rate your skill level, and plan an activity and target date.

Competency	Skill Level		Development Activity	Date
	Current	Desired		

TWO

NAVIGATING COMPANY EXPECTATIONS

Objectives:
- Collect reference material to create your management guidebook
- Understand your organization's expectation of your management role

The Management Map **Reference Pages:** 19-41

Chapter Summary:
The chapter begins with an analogy of how management can be seen as a journey. Typically when people travel they purchase a travel guide book with helpful information that contributes to the enjoyment of their journey. Most of the chapter is dedicated to collecting information to build a management guidebook to include: policy documents, procedure manuals, budget, job descriptions, company objectives, department goals, planning tools, and reference books.

The next section focuses on making sure the new manager understands the expectations of their new role by have a meeting with their manager. Discussion starter questions are provided.

The chapter concludes with a discussion of appropriate workplace attire for managers.

Your Initial Reflection:
What did you like best about the chapter? What topic resonated with you?

_____

_____

_____

Which concepts in the chapter apply to your department or organization?

_____

_____

_____

Which quote did you like from the chapter?

_____

_____

_____

Journey Progress — Check after you complete each activity:

❏ **Activity 2.1: Create Your Management Travel Guidebook** — Gather resources to create a ready reference for frequently utilized information

❏ **Activity 2.2: Utilize Your Management Travel Guidebook** — Use the resources you gathered to answer typical managerial situations

❏ **Activity 2.3: The Expectations Meeting** — Meet with your manager and discuss key issues and challenges for you and your team

❏ **Activity 2.4: Workplace Attire** — Review your company's dress code and analyze whether you need to make adjustments to your attire

Activity 2.1

Create Your Management Travel Guidebook

The Management Map **reference pages 19-30**

Activity Directions: In this activity you will gather information to create a ready reference to quickly access information when a situation arises. The activity includes locating the information, determining who to contact for further information or questions, and deciding on where to store the information for ready reference.

Item	Where to Find It	Contact for More Information	Your Ready Reference Place
1. Company policy manuals including handbooks			
2. Department procedure manuals			
3. Contact information for key individuals			
4. Budget and salary guidelines			
5. Job descriptions for you and your team members			
6. Company vision, mission, values, and objectives			
7. Department goals and objectives			
8. Planning tools available			
9. Reference books			

Activity 2.2

Use Your Management Travel Guidebook
The Management Map reference pages 19-30

Activity Directions: In this activity you will utilize the information you gather for your travel guidebook. After answering these questions, you may decide to store the information differently, gather additional information, or ask for more clarification.

1. Use your company polices and/or handbook to answer these questions:
   a. When are employees eligible to use their vacation or paid time off days?

   _____

   b. Can an employee use a company computer for personal use?

   _____

   c. What do you do if someone complains of being harassed?

   _____

   d. What types of conduct would result in disciplinary action?

   _____

   e. When are performance reviews completed?

   _____

2. What is your budget? Are you authorized to make purchases on behalf of your organization? If yes, up to what limit?

   _____

   _____

   _____

3. What is the procedure for giving one of your team members a raise in salary?

   _____

   _____

   _____

Activity 2.2 Continued

4. What process do you follow if you need to replace a team member?

_____

_____

_____

5. What steps do you take if the fire alarm goes off in the building?

_____

_____

_____

6. Who do you speak to about fixing a computer in your department? What do you do if the computer is beyond repair?

_____

_____

_____

7. How would you explain your company's vision and mission to a new team member?

_____

_____

_____

8. What are the top three goals for your department this year?

_____

_____

_____

Activity 2.3

The Expectations Meeting
The Management Map reference pages 31-37

Activity Directions: To ensure you are spending time on the things critical to your organization, schedule an expectations meeting with your manager. Set an appointment to make sure he/she has adequate time to spend with you. Give thought to and gather as much information as possible before your meeting and be prepared to discuss the following items:

1. What do you see as our key challenges this year? What are the top three things you would like the department to accomplish this year?

_____

_____

_____

_____

2. What barriers do you foresee for us in accomplishing our goals? Do you have recommendations on how we can overcome the barriers?

_____

_____

_____

3. What measurements and milestones are in place?

_____

_____

_____

_____

4. Can you provide me with examples of critical behaviors you would like to see in my department?

_____

_____

_____

Activity 2.3 Continued

5. Are there specific things you would like me to keep in mind when I complete my team members' performance appraisals?

_____

_____

_____

_____

6. How often do you prefer communication from me and by what method?

_____

_____

_____

_____

7. How often would you like an update on goal accomplishments?

_____

_____

_____

_____

8. Is there anything I should know about how you like to work and your behavior expectations for the members of your team that we haven't discussed yet?

_____

_____

_____

_____

9. What are the top three changes you would like to see as a result of this program?

_____

_____

_____

_____

Activity 2.4

Workplace Attire
The Management Map **reference pages 37-39**

Activity Directions: Managers are responsible for administering the company's dress code, so it is critical that the policy is understood and you model the appropriate attire. Complete the following:

1. Locate your company's dress code. List several clothing items that are inappropriate for the workplace.

    _____

    _____

    _____

2. How would you would coach one of your team members who is not dressed appropriately for the office?

    _____

    _____

    _____

3. Observe how several managers in your organization dress. Write down what you observe. Do you have to change your wardrobe to look more like a manager?

    _____

    _____

4. Write down an item of clothing that you will add to your wardrobe and one you will eliminate.

    _____

    _____

5. Team Member Activity: Bring in clothing store flyers and have team members cut out pictures of appropriate and inappropriate workplace attire. Discuss the results of this activity.

    _____

    _____

THREE

GETTING TO KNOW YOUR TRAVELING COMPANIONS

Objectives:
- Gather information about your team members
- Understand team member expectations

The Management Map **Reference Pages:** 43-56

Chapter Summary:
The chapter begins with a story of winning a vacation. The catch: you can only go with people you don't know. It compares getting to know your traveling companions with getting to know your team members because they too are on a journey with you. As a manager you don't accomplish your goals as an individual contributor — you need your team members to be successful.

Everyone comes to the work environment with an expectation of how the work environment should be and how they will be treated. When these expectations are not met, they lead to negative attitudes, job dissatisfaction, decreased productivity, and increased turnover. One way to get to your know team members is to have an open discussion with each of them. Suggested questions are provided to assist with this discussion.

The chapter concludes with a second way to learn more about your team members by conducting a review of their personnel files to develop a snapshot of your team.

Your Initial Reflection:
What did you like best about the chapter? What topic resonated with you?

_____

_____

_____

Which concepts in the chapter apply to your department or organization?

_____

_____

_____

_____

Which quote did you like from the chapter?

_____

_____

_____

Journey Progress — Check after you complete each activity:

☐ **Activity 3.1: Get to Know Your Team Members** — Have a discussion with each of your team members to better be able to adapt your management approach.

☐ **Activity 3.2: Create a Team Snapshot** — Determine the skill and experience level of your team by a review of their files.

Activity 3.1

Get to Know Your Team Members
The Management Map reference pages 47-52

Activity Directions: The more you know about your team members, the better you can adapt your management approach. Have a discussion with your team members to get to know their preferences. Create a note sheet for each employee with their expectations to refer to in the future. *Optional:* Have a role-play practice discussion with a trusted colleague or your manager prior to trying it with your team members. Obtain feedback on your approach.

1. What do you like about our work environment and what would you change?

_____

_____

_____

2. What do you like about the work you do? What do you dislike? How can this activity be changed to make it better for you?

_____

_____

_____

3. What form of communication do you prefer?

_____

_____

_____

4. How do you like to be recognized?

_____

_____

_____

Activity 3.1 Continued

5. What are your future goals? How can I help you achieve your goals? What additional training would you like?

_____

_____

_____

6. Is there anything else you want me, as your manager, to know about what you need to feel successful?

_____

_____

_____

7. Optional: If you and your team members have completed a behavioral profile such as DiSC®, compare your styles.

_____

_____

_____

Questions for discussion:
- What would you do if you can't meet one of your team member's expectations?
- Is it better to have asked or not asked if you can't meet the expectation?

_____

_____

_____

_____

_____

_____

Activity 3.2

Create a Team Snapshot
The Management Map reference pages 53-54

Activity Directions: A good way to determine the skill and experience level of your team is to create a snapshot grid from a review of personnel files. Duplicating a grid such as the one below in spreadsheet application such as Microsoft Excel will allow you to sort, organize, and average data based on what is most relevant to you.

Suggested Columns: The following may be used for ideas of data to collect. You may include as many columns as desired for the specific data you need.

- Number of years with the company
- Education completed and degree
- Number of years in their current position
- Professional certifications

- Number of years of relevant outside experience
- Special skills
- Last performance evaluation

Name	Years w/co.	Yrs in pos.	Years exp.	Ed.	Certif.	Skills	Perf. eval.

How can you use this information to benefit your employees and your department?

FOUR

NO MANAGER IS AN ISLAND

Chapter Learning Points:

- Make a connection with your key contacts
- Utilize collaboration skills with your connections

The Management Map **Reference Pages:** 57-70

Chapter Summary:
The chapter begins with comparing your department to an island. It is important to see your department not as an isolated island but as part of an island chain. Cooperating and collaborating with other departments creates value for the whole company. Collaborating with other departments means learning each other's goals and objectives and how each can contribute to the overall success of the organization.

Discussion questions are provided for meetings with other departments, including support departments, to learn more about their goals and how to better work together.

Understanding and collaborating with external contacts is important too. Discussion questions for analyzing external and internal customers and improving relationships with vendors are included in this chapter.

The chapter concludes with suggestions about how to understand your competition, thereby improving your organization's products and services.

Your Initial Reflection:
What did you like best about the chapter? What topic resonated with you?

_____

_____

_____

Which concepts in the chapter apply to your department or organization?

_____

_____

_____

Which quote did you like from the chapter?

_____

_____

_____

Journey Progress — Check after you complete each activity:

☐ **Activity 4.1: Collaboration Activity Part A** — Analyze the benefits of collaborating with other departments from your perspective and from theirs.

☐ **Activity 4.2: Collaboration Activity Part B** — Reach out to other department managers to discuss their goals and how you can improve collaboration.

☐ **Activity 4.3: Understand Your Customers** — Examine the needs of your internal and external customers.

☐ **Activity 4.4: Develop Customer Empathy** — Brainstorm ways to put yourself in the shoes of the customer so you can better understand his or her viewpoint.

☐ **Activity 4.5: Establish Vendor Expectations** — List and rate your vendors, then discuss how to improve communication and service.

☐ **Activity 4.6: Analyze the Competition** — List and evaluate your organization's competition.

Activity 4.1

Collaboration Activity Part A
The Management Map reference pages 57-63

Activity Directions: This is the first part of a two-part activity focused on collaboration. By collaborating with other departments in your organization, you and your overall organization will achieve better results. Begin this activity by listing other departments and how you would benefit from a more collaborative approach. Now, think about the situation from their perspective and list possible benefits of collaborating for them and their goals and measurements. You may have to leave the last column blank until completing Activity 4.2.

Department	How Collaborating Benefits You	How Collaborating Benefits Them	Their Goals and How They Are Measured

Activity 4.2

Collaboration Activity Part B
The Management Map reference pages 57-63

Activity Directions: This is the second part of a two-part activity focused on collaboration. By collaborating with other departments in your organization, you create a win-win situation that achieves overall better results. Set a meeting with your key contacts. Explain that you want to develop a more collaborative approach that will be of benefit to all. Have a discussion with all of your key contacts to build more collaborative relationships. Ask the questions below but also be prepared to share your answers to the questions. You may duplicate the Activity 4.2 form for every discussion you have with another department manager.

1. How will our collaborating more assist you and your department?

   _____

   _____

   _____

2. What are several goals and objectives for your department?

   _____

   _____

   _____

3. What can my department do to assist you with your goals and objectives?

   _____

   _____

   _____

4. What is your preferred work style? (If you and your colleague have completed a behavioral assessment such as DiSC®, you can compare your profiles.) How do we have to adapt to meet each other's needs?

   _____

   _____

   _____

Activity 4.3

Understand Your Customers
The Management Map reference pages 63-65

Activity Directions: Every organization achieves success by delivering exceptional service to its customers. This activity can be completed individually and/or as a brainstorming session with your team. By involving your team members you are creating a service mindset across your department.

1. Who are your customers, both internal and external?

Internal Customers	External Customers

2. What do your customers want?

Internal Customers	External Customers

3. How do your customers benefit from your service and/or products?

Internal Customers	External Customers

Activity 4.3 Continued

4. What are the consequences of bad service to your customers?

Internal Customers	External Customers

5. List three specific things you can do personally to meet or exceed customer expectations.

Internal Customers	External Customers

6. What specific actions will you take to follow up on ideas from this activity?

_____

_____

_____

_____

_____

Activity 4.4

Develop Customer Empathy
The Management Map **reference pages 63-65**

Activity Directions: When your team members put themselves in the "shoes" of your customers they gain empathy for their needs and requests. Lead a brainstorming session with your team members using these discussion points.

1. Describe the last time you were a customer and received excellent service.

_____

_____

_____

2. List the things the person did that made the service excellent.

_____

_____

_____

3. Pick an item on the previous list, then discuss how to implement it with our customers.

_____

_____

_____

_____

4. Develop specific steps for implementation.

_____

_____

_____

_____

Activity 4.5

Establish Vendor Expectations
The Management Map reference pages 65-66

Activity Directions: The vendors you do business with can be great partners in assisting you in reaching your goals. Begin with a review of the contract or agreement you have with each of your vendors to thoroughly understand what services you are receiving versus what was promised. Then rate the service you are receiving from each of your vendors. Finally, conduct a performance review with each of your vendors in which you share your feedback and create an action plan for the future.

1. List your utilized vendors:

_____

_____

_____

2. Rate each of your vendors in each category from 1 to 5 (5 is highest):

Vendor	Quality	Responsive	Flexibility	Initiative	Value

3. Have a service discussion with your vendors. Begin with what you see as the strengths the vendor provides. Questions and topics can include:

    a. Is there anything else I can do to improve our communications and service?

_____

_____

    b. I would like to see an improvement in _____. Can we discuss possible ways this can be improved?

_____

_____

Activity 4.6

Analyze the Competition
The Management Map **reference pages 66-67**

Activity Directions: Your customers have choices; the choices are what your competitors offer. The purpose of a competitive analysis is to learn from your competitors so that you can adopt their best ideas while ignoring their worst ones. This activity can be completed alone or as a team project.

1. List a few of your major competitors

_____

_____

2. Look up their websites and view them as a potential customer would. What are their strengths and weaknesses?

Competitor	Strength	Weakness

3. If your competitors have retail establishments, make site visits. What are their strengths and weaknesses?

Competitor	Strength	Weakness

4. Based on your analysis, what improvement suggestions do you have for your own organization?

_____

_____

_____

FIVE

SETTING YOUR COURSE AND SPEED

Chapter Learning Points:

- Establish goals for your department and team
- Communicate expectations for your team members

The Management Map Reference Pages: 71-85

Chapter Summary:

The chapter begins with a story about a road trip, introducing the concept of goal setting. Steps for setting goals include determining the goal, resources, plan, milestones, and measurements. These five steps are used in a specific example demonstrating how goals are established in a business setting.

The next section focuses on getting your team members involved in the goal setting process and compares not knowing the department goals to not knowing how to play a game. In order to be successful, team members need to know who is playing, the score, and how to play the game. Discussion starter questions are included to involve team members.

The chapter concludes with explaining your expectations to the team members so no one can say "nobody told me." Suggested items to include in your discussion are new employee orientation information, handbooks/policies, operating procedures, job descriptions, and ground rules.

Your Initial Reflection:

What did you like best about the chapter? What topic resonated with you?

_____

_____

_____

Which concepts in the chapter apply to your department or organization?

_____

_____

_____

Which quote did you like from the chapter?

_____

_____

_____

Journey Progress — Check after you complete each activity:

☐ **Activity 5.1: Goals of the Organization** — Examine the goals of the organization and how your department contributes.

☐ **Activity 5.2: Goal Setting for Your Department** — List a goal for your department based on the process: Goal, Resources, Plan, Milestones, and Measurements.

☐ **Activity 5.3: Involve Your Team in Goal Setting** — Lead a brainstorming session with your team on how to accomplish the goals established in the prior activity.

☐ **Activity 5.4: Establish Expectations for Your Team** — Practice setting expectations with team members utilizing typical company documents.

Activity 5.1

Goals of the Organization
The Management Map reference pages 71-76

Activity Directions: Your goals and the goals of your department contribute to the overall goals of the organization. Locate the goals of your organization and think about how you can make a contribution.

1. List the top three to five strategic initiatives for your organization this year. Then place a check mark next to the top two to three you and your department can impact most.

_____

_____

_____

_____

_____

2. Brainstorm specific actions you and your department can take to contribute to the organization's goals.

_____

_____

_____

_____

_____

_____

_____

_____

_____

_____

Activity 5.2

Goal Setting for Your Department
The Management Map reference pages 71-76

Activity Directions: Effective goal setting involves determining the goal, resources, plan, milestones, and measurements. Pick a goal and complete the following based on examples on pages 74-75. You may duplicate this activity form for every goal.

Goal: State the final result you want to accomplish at the end of the period.

_____

_____

Resources: Make a list of what you have available to accomplish your goal (people, time, money, equipment, space, etc.).

_____

_____

_____

Plan: Write a brief statement about how you will achieve your goal.

_____

_____

Milestones: Identify the interim goals during the period.

_____

_____

_____

Measurements: Answer the question "Was the goal attained?" and estimate what percentage of the goal was completed.

_____

_____

Activity 5.3

Involve Your Team in Goal Setting
The Management Map reference pages 76-80

Activity Directions: Involving your team in goal setting is the first step to gaining their commitment and the eventual success of achieving the goals. Begin by providing everyone with the proposed goals completed in Activity 5.1. Then lead a brainstorming session to gather information about the questions listed below.

1. What additional information would you like to have about our goals?

    _____

    _____

    _____

2. What barriers do you see in our achieving these goals?

    _____

    _____

    _____

3. What suggestions do you have for overcoming the barriers?

    _____

    _____

    _____

4. What recommendations do you have for adjusting our goals up or down? Why should they be adjusted?

    _____

    _____

    _____

5. Are there any other goals we should consider establishing this year? What are they?

    _____

    _____

Activity 5.3 Continued

6. How would these goals contribute to the organization?

_____

_____

_____

Follow-Up Activity Instructions:
This activity's value is maximized by evaluating the information you collect.

Question 1: Here you are soliciting requests for information. If you have the information you can immediately supply it after everyone has a chance to brainstorm items for this question. If you don't have all the information, set a date to give it to them as soon as possible.

Question 3: You identified barriers in question 2. Use a flip chart to list each barrier and leave space next to each to record answers for question 3. In this manner you can handle both questions on the same document. Some barriers will take further investigation to find solutions. Assigning volunteers to investigate and develop solutions increases involvement. Set a date for follow-up when the volunteers will submit their suggestions.

Question 4: You may not be in a position to adjust the goals, but this is still a good question because it may produce additional barriers for research. These barriers can be discussed with your manager who may not have considered the barriers when setting goals.

Questions 5 and 6: It is important to keep your team focused on the overall goals of the organization. If the goals fit with accomplishing the mission and objectives of your company, you should consider adding them or at least provide a well thought out answer as to why they can't be added. You may have to discuss this with your manager before responding, but it is important that you set a date to follow up with your team on a response.

Activity 5.4

Establish Expectations for Your Team
The Management Map reference pages 80-83

Activity Directions: Communicating expectations is like communicating the rules of the game. It's tough to win the game unless you know how to play. You can establish expectations at any time, but it is especially important when a new member joins your team either from outside your company or outside your department. The following is a list of documents you may wish to discuss and space to add your own. Documents come alive with a two-way discussion.

1. **Information from new employee orientation**
   a. What part of orientation did you most enjoy? Least?
   b. Is there any information you wished you had received but didn't?
   c. What questions can I answer?

   _____

   _____

   _____

2. **Handbooks/policies**
   a. What information would you like me to clarify?
   b. I would like to go over a few policies I think are important (make a list before your discussion).

   _____

   _____

   _____

3. **Job descriptions**
   a. What questions do you have about your job description?
   b. Let's go over a few of the key duties and responsibilities.

   _____

   _____

   _____

   _____

Activity 5.4 Continued

4. **Safety policy**
   a. What questions do you have about our safety policies?
   b. Do you know where to report safety and/or accident situations?
   c. Let's go over a few of the key procedures about safety.

   _____

   _____

   _____

5. **Performance appraisal form**
   a. What questions do you have about how you will be evaluated and when?
   b. Let's go over examples of what I'm looking for in each performance category.

   _____

   _____

   _____

6. **Ground rules**
   a. What questions do you have about our team's ground rules?

   _____

   _____

   _____

Establishing Ground Rules: If your team does not have a set of ground rules you can lead a brainstorming discussion to create them. Ground rules govern behavior regarding interaction. They are used to encourage respectful participation. Here are examples of ground rules to get you started:

1. Listen actively: one person talks at a time, no side conversations.
2. Be on time.
3. Respectfully challenge one another by asking questions, but refrain from personal attacks — focus on ideas.
4. Participate to the fullest of your ability.
5. Encourage everyone to participate.
6. Offer solutions, not just problems.
7. Be conscious of body language and nonverbal responses.

SIX

OPENING COMMUNICATION CHANNELS

Chapter Learning Points:

- Target communication to fit the needs of your audience
- Effectively utilize the communication method that best fits the situation

The Management Map **Reference Pages:** 87-103

Chapter Summary:
The chapter begins with a discussion of barriers to effective communication and the importance of communicating from the point of view of your audience. It is important to ask what they want to know, what they need to know, and how they want information to be provided. Examples of how miscommunication occurs are provided.

The remaining content in this chapter discusses tips for communication methods including meetings, one-on-one discussions, e-mail, and instant messaging.

Several key points include creating an agenda for all meetings, assigning roles at meetings, tips to improve listening, ideas to improve e-mail, and the benefits and disadvantages of instant messaging.

Your Initial Reflection:
What did you like best about the chapter? What topic resonated with you?

_____

_____

_____

Which concepts in the chapter apply to your department or organization?

_____

_____

_____

Which quote did you like from the chapter?

_____

_____

_____

Journey Progress — Check after you complete each activity:

☐ **Activity 6.1: Establish Meeting Agendas** — Utilize a template to create an agenda for your next meeting.

☐ **Activity 6.2: Examine Meeting Roles** — Analyze various meeting roles and determine fit for your department.

☐ **Activity 6.3: Choose a Communication Channel** — Choose the best communication method to fit the situation.

Activity 6.1

Establish Meeting Agendas
The Management Map reference pages 92-95

Activity Directions: Your organization may have an established meeting agenda format. If it doesn't, create an agenda template based on the ideas listed below. Your agenda can include the topic arranged by importance and the length of time allocated. Expected outcomes are important to include so everyone is focused on taking action after the meeting. Circulating the agenda prior to the meeting will ensure everyone is focused on the topics and brings relevant documents and ideas. Create an agenda for your next meeting and get feedback from participants.

Meeting Title: _____

Date: _____

Start and End Time: _____

Location: _____

Meeting Facilitator: _____

(Name and contact information)

AGENDA

Length	Topic	Responsible	Action*

*Decision, Vote, Ideas, Discussion, Information

Action Plan (information to be reviewed at the close of the meeting):

Action	Responsible	Date Due

Activity 6.2

Examine Meeting Roles
The Management Map reference pages 92-95

Activity Directions: The attendees of your meeting may benefit from having assigned roles at meetings. These roles can be rotated to give everyone an opportunity to participate. Examine the following typical meeting roles and add or delete other roles as appropriate:

- **Facilitator**: Keeps the discussion flowing based on the agenda, encourages everyone's participation, and resolves conflict.

  ☐ Currently utilize this role   ☐ Add this role   ☐ Change this role by:

  _____

  _____

- **Timekeeper**: Monitors the time allotted for the meeting and each agenda item. Notifies presenters when their time is about to end and the whole group when the meeting is coming to a close.

  ☐ Currently utilize this role   ☐ Add this role   ☐ Change this role by:

  _____

  _____

- **Note Taker**: Takes legible notes for later review and reference. May also be asked to distribute notes after the meeting to the attendees.

  ☐ Currently utilize this role   ☐ Add this role   ☐ Change this role by:

  _____

  _____

- **Presenter**: A content expert who delivers information or leads a discussion as part of the agenda.

  ☐ Currently utilize this role   ☐ Add this role   ☐ Change this role by:

  _____

  _____

Activity 6.2 Continued

- **Coordinator**: Arranges for the meeting location logistics, equipment needed, handouts, refreshments, etc.

  ☐ Currently utilize this role   ☐ Add this role   ☐ Change this role by:

  _____

  _____

- **Attendee**: Focuses on the agenda and willingly offers contributions.

  ☐ Currently utilize this role   ☐ Add this role   ☐ Change this role by:

  _____

  _____

- **Other Role**: _____

  ☐ Currently utilize this role   ☐ Add this role   ☐ Change this role by:

  _____

  _____

- **Other Role**: _____

  ☐ Currently utilize this role   ☐ Add this role   ☐ Change this role by:

  _____

  _____

Activity 6.3

Choose a Communication Channel
The Management Map reference pages 87-101

Activity Directions: It is important to determine the method of communication that fits the situation. Review the list below and then complete the exercise as indicated. Match the following types of messages with the appropriate communication method by indicating **A** for One-on-One, **B** for Written, or **C** for Group Meeting.

Method	Situation Type
A. One-on-One communication	• Need for quick information • Private conversations
B. Written communication (letters, e-mails, etc.)	• For very detailed information • A record of information is required
C. Group Meeting	• Group participation required • Information needed by everyone

Type of Message	A, B, or C
1. Coaching on absenteeism	
2. Department results for the month	
3. New procedures for testing quality	
4. Performance appraisals	
5. Abuse of break times	
6. Resolving a dispute	
7. New employee introduction	
8. New customer announcement	
9. Productivity statistics for the month	
10. Disciplinary discussion	
11. Meeting schedule for the month	
12. Individual recognition	
13. Brainstorm solutions to a department problem	
14. Respond to an e-mail requesting more information	
15. Recognition for a group accomplishment	

SEVEN

GUIDING THE JOURNEY

Chapter Learning Points:

- Create a positive work climate
- Develop a coaching mindset

The Management Map **Reference Pages:** 105-123

Chapter Summary:
The chapter begins with a comparison of a manager to a ship's captain. Managers set the course, provide course corrections, build a positive workplace climate, and create satisfaction for employees and customers.

Creating a positive work climate contributes to employee retention, productivity, innovation, and teamwork. Three new concepts are discussed in addition to a summary of concepts from other chapters demonstrating how managers can create a positive work climate. Involvement of team members is important, and several discussion starting questions are included in the chapter.

The remainder of the chapter focuses on the "coaching mindset," which involves thinking positive thoughts about your team members, feeling that you want the best from your team members, and acting in such a way that your team members believe that you want the best for them. Two techniques are discussed: MBWA (Management by Walking Around) and feedback skills.

Your Initial Reflection:
What did you like best about the chapter? What topic resonated with you?

_____

_____

_____

Which concepts in the chapter apply to your department or organization?

_____

_____

_____

Which quote did you like from the chapter?

_____

_____

_____

Journey Progress — Check after you complete each activity:

☐ **Activity 7.1: Rate Your Work Climate** — Analyze your work climate based on five categories.

☐ **Activity 7.2: Improve Your Work Climate** — Create an action plan with your team on one category from the prior activity during a brainstorming session.

☐ **Activity 7.3: Examine Your Thoughts** — Analyze how your initial thoughts impact your approach to coaching.

☐ **Activity 7.4: Rate Your Coaching Skills** — Use the provided skill list to help determine your strengths and weaknesses as a coach.

☐ **Activity 7.5: Practice Coaching I** — Choose a sample situation a manager may encounter in the workplace and practice the coaching skills needed to resolve the situation.

☐ **Activity 7.6: Practice Coaching II** — Use the same skills and process to plan a coaching session for an actual workplace situation.

Activity 7.1

Rate Your Work Climate
The Management Map reference pages 105-109

Activity Directions: A positive work climate leads to employee motivation, performance, retention, and engagement. Your organization may already conduct a climate survey. If it doesn't, rate it using the key below and provide a specific example.
Key:
1 = Consistently present in the environment
2 = Present most of the time
3 = Occasionally present
4 = Normally not present in the environment

1. (   ) Positive work relationship with team members. Example:

_____

_____

2. (   ) Open communication channels. Example:

_____

_____

3. (   ) Established goals and expectations. Example:

_____

_____

4. (   ) Trust among team members. Example:

_____

_____

5. (   ) Use a benefit-of-the-doubt approach. Example:

_____

_____

Activity 7.2

Improve Your Work Climate
The Management Map reference pages 105-109

Activity Directions: As stated in Activity 7.1, a positive work climate leads to employee motivation, performance, retention, and engagement. Your organization may already conduct a climate survey. If that is the case, use the categories from your survey to brainstorm ideas with your team on how to improve the work climate in your area. If you don't have a climate survey, use the categories from Activity 7.1 to brainstorm with your team members. Break your employees into smaller teams and assign one category to each. Distribute these actionable items to all participants. Review progress at periodic meetings.

Category
- Positive work relationship with team members
- Open communication channels
- Established goals and expectations
- Trust among team members
- Use a benefit-of-the-doubt approach

Key
1 = Consistently present in the environment
2 = Present most of the time
3 = Occasionally present
4 = Normally not present in the environment

Provide a handout or flip chart similar to the following for each team.

Category assigned:
Rating (*Refer to key*):
Give a specific example of how this is currently demonstrated in our department:
List three actionable items that can be done to improve this category:

Activity 7.3

Examine Your Thoughts
The Management Map reference pages 109-113

Activity Directions: Fill in the blanks with your first thoughts after reading the following sentence openings. Then answer the debrief questions below.

People are... _____

Employees are... _____

New employees are... _____

Managers are... _____

Coaching is... _____

Discipline is... _____

1. Which of your answers surprised you?

_____

_____

2. Were your sentences the same or different for "Employees are..." and "New employees are..."?

_____

_____

3. How do you think your answers will impact the way you approach coaching?

_____

_____

_____

Activity 7.4

Rate Your Coaching Skills
The Management Map **reference pages 113-115**

Activity Directions: The following list of skills is frequently utilized by effective coaches with their team members. Rate your skills on the scale of 1-4, with 4 being the highest.

Skill	1	2	3	4
1. Openly share information				
2. Provide frequent feedback				
3. Feedback provided is both positive and negative				
4. Demonstrate patience				
5. Effectively listen and clarify understanding				
6. Quickly assess off-track performance				
7. Provide recognition for accomplishments				
8. Available to answer questions and concerns				
9. Remove obstacles that interfere with team members success				
10. Appear approachable and not "bothered" by questions				
11. Provide early feedback before problems become severe				

What is your greatest strength?

_____

Give an example of how you have successfully used this skill:

_____

_____

List one skill that could be improved and an action plan for improvement:

_____

_____

Activity 7.5

Practice Coaching I
The Management Map reference pages 109-118

Activity Directions: Choose one of the situations listed below and prepare and practice a coaching session. You may have to elaborate by adding related facts.

Situation 1: Patti is a customer service representative. She is technically proficient in her knowledge of procedures and systems. You have observed Patti raising her voice when speaking to customers who appear to frustrate her. Not only have customers complained, but her behavior appears to disturb others in her area who can't hear their own phone calls.

Situation 2: Michele is an accounts clerk. She is a great asset to the team; always cheerful and willing to help others. The spreadsheets she completes are not always accurate and require several revisions before they meet standards. Michele has also made errors in her other tasks.

Situation 3: Stu is a sales representative. He is great at multi-tasking, closes deals, and uses excellent interpersonal skills with clients and team members. He is required as part of his job to complete status reports. Unfortunately, either the reports don't get done without a reminder from you or are turned in about a week late.

1. What are your employee's strengths? List compliments about the strengths.

_____

_____

_____

2. Provide a specific example of an area in need of improvement.

_____

_____

_____

3. Explain the impact of the behavior or performance issue.

_____

_____

_____

Activity 7.5 Continued

4. List questions that will identify barriers to success and eventually to a solution.

_____

_____

_____

_____

5. Ask your team member for a solution.

_____

_____

_____

_____

6. Plan a follow up date and time.

_____

_____

Additional Activity Direction: After planning your discussion, locate two volunteers to practice with you; one to play the role of your team member and one to play an observer who will take notes on the following page and provide you feedback.

Activity 7.5 Continued

Observer Feedback Sheet

Activity Directions: Complete this feedback sheet for one of the members of your table team as they practice their coaching situation.

	Excellent	Good Job	Needs Work
Helpful tone and body language			
Valued team member strengths			
Provided specific feedback with examples			
Explained importance			
Asked questions to determine barriers to performance			
Used a problem solving approach			
Created follow up action plans			

Ideas for Improvement: _____

_____

_____

_____

Activity 7.6

Practice Coaching II
The Management Map **reference pages 109-118**

Activity Directions: After completing Activity 7.5 with a supplied situation, you are now ready to practice your own situation. Think of a situation involving one of your team members and complete the process below.

1. What are your employee's strengths? List compliments about the strengths.

_____

_____

_____

2. Provide a specific example of an area in need of improvement.

_____

_____

3. Explain the impact of the behavior or performance issue.

_____

_____

_____

4. List questions that will identify barriers to success and eventually to a solution.

_____

_____

_____

_____

5. Ask your team member for a solution.

_____

_____

_____

Activity 7.6 Continued

6. Plan a follow up date and time.

_____

_____

Additional Activity Direction: After planning your discussion, locate two volunteers to practice with you; one to play the role of your team member and one to play an observer who will take notes and give you feedback. Since you are now discussing a real employee, change the name and discuss the importance of confidentiality.

EIGHT

GETTING THERE ON TIME...
Time Management Tips

Objectives:
- Spend your time on managerial activities
- Develop effective time management techniques

The Management Map **Reference Pages:** 125-141

Chapter Summary:
The chapter focuses on appropriate time management for managers. The question is asked "How are you spending your time?" which can be answered by completing a time log. Several examples of how managers typically spend their time are provided.

A typical danger many managers face is holding on to tasks and activities they did prior to becoming a manager. The ATES — delegate, automate, and eliminate — are discussed as solutions to this typical situation.

The chapter concludes with four areas of time management that managers need to develop. Tips and techniques are discussed in each of these areas.

Your Initial Reflection:
What did you like best about the chapter? What topic resonated with you?

_____

_____

_____

Which concepts in the chapter apply to your department or organization?

_____

_____

_____

Which quote did you like from the chapter?

_____

_____

_____

Journey Progress — Check after you complete each activity:

❐ **Activity 8.1: Complete a Time Log** — Pick several dates and write down everything you do.

❐ **Activity 8.2: Analyze Your Time Log** — Analyze your time log to determine your percent of managerial activities and how to best manage interruptions.

❐ **Activity 8.3: Project Planning** — Use a worksheet to begin planning the steps of a project.

Activity 8.1

Complete a Time Log
The Management Map reference pages 125-128

Activity Directions: Managers spend their time differently than individual contributors. What does a manager do all day? To find out what you do, choose a typical day and write everything you do next to the time. Just list your tasks, the other columns will be discussed in future activities.

TIME LOG Example

Daily Time Log						
Name:			Date:			
Time	Activity	Management /Individual		Possible Solutions		
				Delegate	Automate	Eliminate
7:00		M	I			
		M	I			
7:30		M	I			
		M	I			
8:00	Greeted all team members, discussed	M	I			
	their priorities for the day	M	I			
8:30		M	I			
		M	I			
9:00	Read e-mail	M	I			

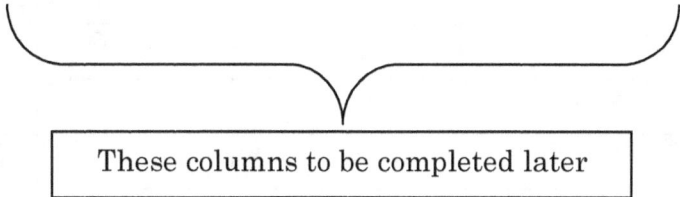

These columns to be completed later

TIME LOG

Daily Time Log					
Name:		Date:			
Time	Activity	Management /Individual	Possible Solutions		
			Delegate	Automate	Eliminate
7:00		M I			
		M I			
7:30		M I			
		M I			
8:00		M I			
		M I			
8:30		M I			
		M I			
9:00		M I			
		M I			
9:30		M I			
		M I			
10:00		M I			
		M I			
10:30		M I			
		M I			
11:00		M I			
		M I			
11:30		M I			
		M I			
12:00		M I			
		M I			
12:30		M I			
		M I			

TIME LOG (Continued)

Daily Time Log						
Name:			Date:			
Time	Activity	Management/ Individual		Possible Solutions		
				Delegate	Automate	Eliminate
1:00		M	I			
		M	I			
1:30		M	I			
		M	I			
2:00		M	I			
		M	I			
2:30		M	I			
		M	I			
3.00		M	I			
		M	I			
3:30		M	I			
		M	I			
4:00		M	I			
		M	I			
4:30		M	I			
		M	I			
5:00		M	I			
		M	I			
5:30		M	I			
		M	I			
6:00		M	I			
		M	I			
6:30		M	I			
		M	I			

Activity 8.2

Analyze Your Time Log
The Management Map reference pages 127-138

Activity Directions: Analyze your time log and answer the following questions:

1. Examine all your tasks and circle whether they were (M) managerial tasks or (I) individual contributor tasks. What percentage of time was spent on managerial tasks? What percent is appropriate for your role? Share the findings with your manager and ask him/her the appropriate percent from his/her perspective.

Percentage managerial:

Percentage individual:

Is this percentage appropriate for your role?

2. Examine your time log for possible tasks that can be delegated, automated, or eliminated.

Delegate	Automate	Eliminate

3. How many times were you interrupted during the day? What was the nature of the interruptions? Do the interruptions indicate a need for additional training or empowerment?

Activity 8.2 Continued

4. How much time was spent in meetings? Were all the meetings appropriate or could the information have been handled with another communication method? Were all the meetings well organized or should they have been shorter?

_____

_____

_____

_____

_____

5. The following are typical managerial tasks. Check the tasks that appeared on your time log:

☐ Give instructions   ☐ Set goals

☐ Train/develop   ☐ Discuss policies

☐ Coach   ☐ Delegate

☐ Plan   ☐ Review performance

☐ Create procedures   ☐ Recognize

☐ Give feedback   ☐ Problem solve

☐ Lead meetings   ☐ Manage projects

☐ Monitor work   ☐ Discipline

☐ Resolve complaints   ☐ Interview

☐ Manage conflict   ☐ Manage budgets

6. What other insights did your time log reveal?

_____

_____

_____

_____

Activity 8.3

Project Planning
The Management Map reference pages 138-139

Activity Directions: Many tasks assigned to managers are long term and require good project management skills. If you are accustomed to completing all your work in one day, this may seem overwhelming without a plan.

Project plans are great tools to help organize the tasks of your project and set milestones to measure your progress. You can purchase a project management software program, utilize an electronic spreadsheet such as Excel, or simply create columns on a piece of paper.

The form on the following page (sometimes known as a work breakdown structure) is a sample you can duplicate on paper or in a spreadsheet. If you currently have a project, fill out the form with the information you currently have. Work with your manager and others to complete the rest. Here are the steps:

1. Begin by brainstorming all the tasks and subtasks required to complete the project. Don't try to put them in order now. Doing so may stifle your creativity.

2. Put the tasks in logical order by adding a number in the column labeled #.

3. Add a time-to-complete column next to each task. Time to complete can be days, weeks, months, etc.; whatever time frame is the most appropriate for your project. By totaling this column you will have an estimate of how long the total project will take.

4. Select the logical person or persons who will complete each task and add their initials to the worksheet. This person can also be you.

5. Estimate the dollar amount needed for all the resources needed to complete the tasks, including money, equipment, materials, etc.

6. Total the amount to establish the budget.

7. Communicate the plan to your manager and team and ask for his or her input on time and resources.

8. Adjust the plan based on any new information received.

9. Obtain approval for the budget and time frame to complete based on resources needed.

10. Monitor and report progress.

11. Celebrate success.

Project Plan

#	Task/Subtask	Time Req.	Initials	Equip. $	Material $	Salary $	Travel $	Other $

NINE

LICENSE TO MANAGE...
Employment Law Awareness

Chapter Learning Points:

- Understand that employment laws protect employees' rights
- Focus on simple rules for managers to avoid violating employment laws

***The Management Map* Reference Pages:** 143-158

Chapter Summary:
The chapter is devoted to awareness of employment laws and the rights of employees. Rights of employees include the right to be free from discrimination, the right to a safe environment, the right to be paid for hours worked, the right to job protection, and the right to file a complaint.

Managers are the company in the eyes of the law and therefore are in a position of incurring substantial costs for the organization if employment laws are violated. Manager employment law basics are provided.

The chapter concludes with five workplace situations that managers may encounter. Issues to consider are listed after each situation.

Your Initial Reflection:
What did you like best about the chapter? What topic resonated with you?

_____

_____

_____

Which concepts in the chapter apply to your department or organization?

_____

_____

_____

Which quote did you like from the chapter?

_____

_____

_____

Journey Progress — Check after you complete each activity:

☐ **Activity 9.1: Review Federal Agency Websites** — Become familiar with the websites that offer information about federal employment law.

☐ **Activity 9.2: Respond to Employee Situations** — Analyze situations that may occur in the workplace related to employment law.

☐ **Activity 9.3: Practice Employee Situations** — Role play two of the situations from Activity 9.2.

Activity 9.1

Review Federal Agency Websites
The Management Map reference pages 144-150

Activity Directions: Following is a list of federal agency websites that provide information or forms for filing complaints by employees. Go to each website and write down one or two interesting facts that you learn.

Equal Employment Opportunity Commission (EEOC) — www.EEOC.gov

_____

_____

_____

_____

Department of Labor (DOL) — www.DOL.gov

_____

_____

_____

_____

Occupational Safety and Health Administration (OSHA) — www.OSHA.gov

_____

_____

_____

_____

National Labor Relations Board (NLRB) — www.NLRB.gov

_____

_____

_____

_____

Activity 9.2

Respond to Employee Situations
The Management Map **reference pages 143-155**

Activity Directions: Managers are in the workplace making decisions on the spot, so it is important that they have at least a basic understanding of the rights of their employees. Read the situations below and answer the questions that follow. Your company policies may assist you in answering the questions. When you complete each situation, discuss your answers with a higher level manager or human resources professional.

1. A team member tells you that she has to take off every other week for four hours, over the next three months, to take her mother to radiation therapy. **Issues to consider:**
   a) How will you respond to the team member?
   b) Is this a "right to job protection" situation?
   c) How will the team member be paid?
   d) Is there a request form to take the time off?

   a) _____

   b) _____

   c) _____

   d) _____

2. During an employment interview, a candidate suddenly shares that she is single mom with three children and must stay home with them when they are ill. **Issues to consider:**
   a) How will you respond to the candidate?
   b) Do you consider this unsolicited information when you make your hiring decision?
   c) Is this a "right to be free from discrimination" situation?

   a) _____

   b) _____

   c) _____

Activity 9.2 Continued

3. You pass an employee's workstation and see a sexually explicit website on his computer. The employee sees your look of horror and says: "I'm on my lunch break." **Issues to consider:**
    a) How will you respond to the team member?
    b) What policies exist on harassment and personal use of company equipment?
    c) Is this a "right to be free from discrimination situation"?

    a) _____

    b) _____

    c) _____

4. An overtime eligible employee, who is very dedicated, offers to work an extra two hours to finish an important report. She says: "I know we don't have overtime in the budget, so don't worry about paying me." **Issues to consider:**
    a) How will you respond to the team member?
    b) How will you get the report completed if the team member doesn't work the extra hours?
    c) Is this a "right to be paid for hours worked" situation?

    a) _____

    b) _____

    c) _____

5. An employee passes you in the hallway, rubbing his elbow. When you ask him what is wrong he says he fell in the lunch room, but he's okay, no need to report it or fill out any forms. **Issues to consider:**
    a) How will you respond to the team member?
    b) What are the consequences of not reporting an on-the-job injury?
    c) Is this a "right to a safe environment" situation?

    a) _____

    b) _____

    c) _____

Activity 9.3

Practice Employee Situations
The Management Map **reference pages 143-155**

Activity Directions: After you confirm that your answers are correct according to the law and company policy, it is time to practice what you would say in each situation. Pick two of the situations from Activity 9.2 and plan a role play practice. Locate two volunteers to practice with you; one to play the role of your team member and one to play an observer who will take notes and give you feedback.

Situation 1
What you will say:

_____

_____

_____

_____

What your team member will say:

_____

_____

_____

_____

Situation 2
What you will say:

_____

_____

_____

_____

What your team member will say:

_____

_____

_____

_____

TEN

NAVIGATING ROADBLOCKS, DETOURS, AND SPEED BUMPS

Chapter Learning Points:

- Identify situations that disrupt your management journey
- Overcome obstacles with practical tips and techniques

The Management Map **Reference Pages:** 159-170

Chapter Summary:

The chapter discusses the things that can go wrong during your management journey: roadblocks, detours, and speed bumps.

Road blocks are situations or conditions that prevent you from progressing toward accomplishment of your goals. Five problem-solving steps are outlined to use when encountering a road block instead of "going down the road of resentment."

A detour is a metaphor for dealing with organizational change. Managers must perform the role of change agent during times of transition. Five steps are outlined that provide suggestions on how to manage change.

The chapter concludes with a discussion of speed bumps, which are conflicts in the workplace. Six practical tips are provided for dealing with conflict and searching for a win-win solution.

Your Initial Reflection:

What did you like best about the chapter? What topic resonated with you?

_____

_____

_____

Which concepts in the chapter apply to your department or organization?

_____

_____

_____

Which quote did you like from the chapter?

_____

_____

_____

Journey Progress — Check after you complete each activity:

☐ **Activity 10.1: Navigate a Roadblock** — Apply steps for handling a situation in which you are not able to progress toward a goal.

☐ **Activity 10.2: Analyze an Organizational Change** — Describe a recent change situation and answer questions to be able to implement the change.

☐ **Activity 10.3: Analyze a Conflict Situation** — Think about a recent conflict situation at work and objectively analyze for resolution.

Activity 10.1

Navigating a Roadblock
The Management Map reference pages 159-162

Activity Directions: A roadblock is a situation or condition that prevents you from progressing toward an accomplishment of your goals. The following are situations that may occur in the workplace. Choose a situation, or make up one of your own, and apply steps 1-5 to navigating a roadblock.

- Your budget gets cut
- You lose a key member of your team
- You temporarily lose a key member of your team through an extended illness
- Technology resources are limited
- Your manager doesn't approve your project plan
- You have to lay off a team member

1. Determine the current reality of the situation (not what you wish it was!).

_____

_____

_____

2. Brainstorm possible solutions.

_____

_____

_____

3. Choose a solution based on logical criteria.

_____

_____

4. Create a new plan.

_____

_____

_____

Activity 10.1 Continued

5. Who needs to learn of the plan? Design an effective communication of the plan.

_____

_____

_____

_____

Activity 10.2

Analyze an Organizational Change
The Management Map **reference pages 162-165**

Activity Directions: Organizations are always going to be faced with change due to the impact of external forces and internal desires for continuous improvement. It is important that managers perform the role of change agent during times of transition. Start this activity by identifying a recent organizational change, then complete each section below. Pages 164 and 165 will be especially helpful in this activity.

Change Situation:

_____

_____

1. Identify what exactly is changing and why.

_____

_____

_____

2. How will you plan the change?

_____

_____

_____

3. How will you communicate the change?

_____

_____

_____

4. How will you encourage involvement in the change?

_____

_____

_____

Activity 10.2 Continued

5. How will you adapt to the needs of your team members? List each of your team members and the approach you will use to assist them in adapting to the change.

Name	Approach

Activity 10.3

Analyze a Conflict Situation
The Management Map reference pages 165-168

Activity Directions: Conflict is inevitable because it is extremely unlikely that two or more people working closely together every day would not disagree on something. Start this activity by identifying a recent conflict and then complete each section below. The conflict could be your own or one that you had to mediate as a manager.

1. What were the objective reasons for the conflict? (Examples include responsibility overlap or gaps, conflicting goals and objectives, competition over scarce resources, etc.)

_____

_____

_____

2. What was each person's natural response to conflict?

Negative Responses	Positive Responses
• Becomes aggressive and autocratic	• Discusses tough issues
• Personally attacks	• Communicates empathy
• Overpowers with logic and facts	• Problem solves to find the facts
• Accommodates or gives in	• Looks for a "win-win" solution

_____

_____

_____

3. Ask "What do we already know about the situation and what don't we know?"

_____

_____

4. Brainstorm solutions to the conflict. Ask "How can we prevent this from happening again?"

_____

_____

_____

Final Activity

Action Plan

Activity Directions: Flip through *The Management Map Companion Workbook* to review all the concepts we discussed. Develop your plan of action for implementation. You may wish to review what was discussed during question 9 in Activity 2.3: The Expectations Meeting, with your manager.

1. Key Concept: _____
Specific Actions I will take:

_____

_____

_____

_____

2. Key Concept: _____
Specific Actions I will take:

_____

_____

_____

_____

3. Key Concept: _____
Specific Actions I will take:

_____

_____

_____

_____

RESOURCES FOR YOUR MANAGEMENT JOURNEY

Visit www.TheManagementMap.com
Additional Resources, Ongoing Discussions and More!

Management Skills Resource, Inc. is your resource for all your management development training needs. Our products and services are dedicated to the advancement and on-the-job application of effective management principles.

Building the *competence*, *confidence,* and *courage* of your management teams through:

Classroom Training — Using proven templates, we custom design workshops based on your company's culture, policies and procedures.

On-Line Training — Each on-line course contains interactive exercises, simulations, and assessment tools, including a pre and post test so that it's easy to measure knowledge acquisition.

Assessment Tools — Our learning instruments are always designed to align people's skills and behavior with organizational strategies.

Management Skills Resource, Inc.

www.ManagementSkillsResource.com
Info@ManagementSkillsResource

About the Author

Deborah Avrin, MS, SPHR, brings over 20 years of human resources and training experience to her company, Management Skills Resource, Inc. Her coaching skills have assisted countless managers to improve their performance in such diverse industries as financial services, manufacturing, utilities, transportation, education, non-profit and telecommunications.

Prior to beginning her consulting practice in 1998, Deborah Avrin held a variety of top-level human resources leadership positions in both the financial services and manufacturing industries. She also has held operational management positions, which enables her to understand the unique training needs of managers. Her reputation is as a motivator, with an inspiring training style that encourages others to excel.

Her company, Management Skills Resource, Inc., works with organizations that want to build the confidence, competence and courage of their management teams through creative training workshops.

Her educational background includes a BBA in human resources and a masters degree in organizational behavior. Deborah Avrin also holds a lifetime Senior Professional in Human Resources (SPHR) certification.

www.ingramcontent.com/pod-product-compliance
Lightning Source LLC
Chambersburg PA
CBHW082106210326
41599CB00033B/6612